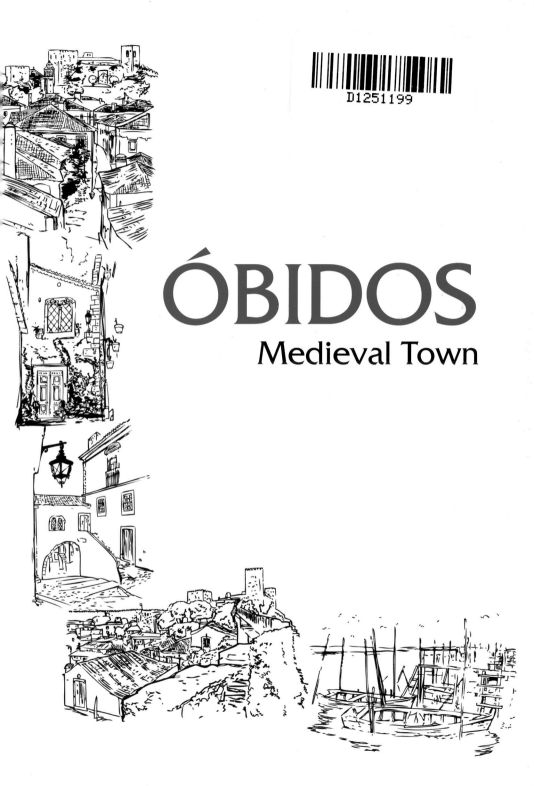

ÓBIDOS
Medieval Town

Bibliography

"Óbidos Vila Museu" - Joaquim da Silveira Botelho
"Óbidos, Arquitectura e Urbanismo Séculos XVI e XVII"
Teresa Bettencourt da Câmara

EDITOR

Vitor Vieira
PUBLICAÇÕES

www.vitorvieira.net
fotografia@vitorvieira.net

Original idea, historical research, photographs and artwork by
Vitor Vieira

Illustrations by
www.karikamania.no.sapo.pt

Printing and image processing by
DPI Cromotipo, Lisbon
geral@dpicromotipo.pt

Translation
Alan Jones
alanjonestranslator@gmail.com

This booklet is also available in
French, German, Italian, Japanese, Portuguese and Spanish,

Legal deposit no.: 278910/08
ISBN: 978-972-8264-36-9

HISTORY

The origins of Óbidos are lost in the mists of time.

Archaeological works in Outeiro da Assenta suggest that it has been inhabited since very early times.

Several historians date the town's origin to the times of the Turdulos and Celts who built massive, protective walls, sometime around the year 308 bc.

Óbidos's name appears to derive from the Latin OB-ID-OS, owing to the existence, many years ago of a sea inlet which extended up to as far as the town itself, although this etymology has been contested. Several people consider that it may have been built on top of a Portuguese-Roman OPPIDUM [1]

Several sections of the wall appear to date from the Roman occupation.

Óbidos bears traces of the Alans, Suevi, Visigoths and Arabs.

Gonçalo Mendes da Maia, the governor general of Afonso Henriques, put an end to the hegemony of the Arabs, on 11 January 1148, when he took the town after putting down strong resistance.

Óbidos won the favour of the kings of the "Afonsine" dynasty. Its reconstruction and enlargement were commissioned by Afonso Henriques.

When taking up residence, in 1186, Sancho I, fortified the town and increased its number of inhabitants.

Afonso II gave the town to his consort Urraca, as a present, on 7 December 1210.

Sancho II, at odds with both clergy and nobility, lived in Óbidos for a short period around 1224. He was accompanied by a large number of followers who, together with Lady Mécia and other dames and damsels comprised the royal court.

Afonso, Count of Bologne, who was later to become Afonso III, laid siege to Óbidos for eight months. The knight courtier Fernando Ourigues de Aboim, together with Vasco Moniz and Gonçalo de Sequeira and other nobles, had defended Sancho II's rights in refusing to swear allegiance to the "Bolognese".

The inhabitants, aided by Friar Pedro Gonçalves, Abbot of Alcobaça, put up stiff resistance.

Afonso III, after his coronation granted Óbidos several privileges, benefits and the title of semper fidelis, together with its existing title of most noble.

Dinis gave his consort, Isabel (the "Queen Saint"), title to Óbidos under the terms of a royal charter, as a wedding present, after having enlarged the town and rebuilt its castle, in addition to other towns. It then became the property of the Casa das Rainhas ("House of the Queens") which was extinguished in 1834.

Inês de Castro remained secluded in the castle, in the last few years of the reign of Afonso IV.

The castle was refurbished at the behest of the last king of the first dynasty who commissioned the building of its keep, repaired its walls and donated the town to his consort Leonor Teles.

Óbidos remained in the possession of the Casa das Rainhas and became the property of Philippa of Lancaster. João I changed the Roman calendar to the Christian calendar on 12 August 1427.

It was in Óbidos that King Duarte is thought

Royal Charter

to have written *"A arte de bem cavalgar toda a sela"*[2].

Afonso V married Queen Isabel at the *Igreja de Santa Maria (" Saint Mary's Church")*.

Eleanor of Lancaster was deeply shaken by the death of her son, Afonso, in 1491 and founded the *Misericórdia do Reino* (charitable institution) in the *Capela do Espírito Santo* ("Chapel of the Holy Spirit"), in 1498, to which she contributed generously.

The "Queen Saint" granted Óbidos a royal charter[3] in 1326. A new charter was granted by King Manuel, on 20 August 1513, who appears to have commissioned the castle's last refurbishment.

Catherine of Austria, spouse of João III, ordered the construction of an aqueduct.

João III was responsible for setting up the *Casa do Estudante* ("House of Students") and establishing a chair in mathematics, which was later to be replaced by a chair in theology.

King Sebastião's reign was marked by the disastrous expedition to Alcácer-Quibir, in which Afonso de Noronha and a large number of nobles from the municipal district, together with around five hundred soldiers on foot and horseback, met their end.

Filipe III raised Óbidos to a county seat, in 1634, under the stewardship of Vasco de Mascarenhas.

The construction of the *Casa da Câmara* (town hall), which was, until recently, a jail and which currently houses the municipal museum, was commissioned during the period of residence in Óbidos of João IV and his consort Luiza de Gusmão, after the Restoration[4].

The *Santuário do Senhor da Pedra* was built owing to the king's generous gifts of income and benefits in kind.

A large proportion of the town's buildings and churches was destroyed in the 1755 earthquake.

The Count of Óbidos ordered reconstruction works to be carried out on the *Paços da Cerca* (palace), *Igreja de S. Tiago* (Saint James's Church) and *Igreja de S. Pedro* (Saint Peter's Church), the Barbican Tower and a section of the western walls.

Maria I and her consort Pedro II, took up residence in Óbidos owing to the outbreak of an epidemic in Caldas da Rainha. The occasion was commemorated by two coats-of-arms, set above the main door of the *Solar da Praça da Rainha* (manor house) and which is currently owned by the municipality.

---

[1] *OPPIDUM - an urban centre or fortified city*
[2] *A famous treatise on horseriding*
[3] *Granting authority to administer a location or municipal district.*
[4] *A period of war between Portugal and Spain for the restoration of the independence of mainland Portugal (1641-1668).*

CASTLE

The castle was built in Roman times on top of a crag. It was used by the Saracens as a fortress over the years.

The castle is a highly exquisite, perfect specimen of a medieval fortress which was successively enlarged and repaired by the monarchs of the first dynasty. It is protected by a long wall which afforded the town both shelter and protection.

João de Noronha provided the castle's interior with a palace-type ambience.

King Manuel commissioned refurbishing works, in the early 16th century, in addition to fortifying the castle's defensive perimeter.

The castle has ornate, *Manueline* architectural style windows and a veranda.

It currently houses a *pousada* (state inn).

1 *Manueline window*
2 *Pousada (housed in Castle)*

1

2

WALLS

The walls are 1,565 metres long, are easily accessible and provide a pleasant stroll.

A visitor enters Óbidos via four gateways and two archways.

Refurbishment works were commissioned by several monarchs, including Afonso Henriques, Sancho I, Diniz and Fernando.

The northern walls are reinforced by the castle proper and the southern walls by the *Torre do Facho* (torch-lit watchtower).

Special reference should be made to the entrance to the town with its oratory chapel, lined with highly ornamental 18th century tiles.

1 *Postigo do Arrabalde (archway)*
2 *Walls, part view of Óbidos and Torre do Facho*
3 *Capela da Nossa Senhora da Piedade*
   (Chapel of Our Lady of Piety)
4 *Walls, part view of Óbidos*

CLOCK
OR BARBICAN TOWER

The clock, or barbican tower, was commissioned by King Sancho. The machinery was installed in the clock tower (from which its name derived), in 1842, known as the Barbican (owing to the fact that this was the depository for the crown jewels).

It was later to be used as a prison.

Castilian chronicler, politician, diplomat and scholar, Pedro Lopes de Ayalla was imprisoned in the tower for a period of 15 months, after the battle of Aljubarrota[1]. It was here that he wrote several of his best poems.

[1] *Battle of Aljubarrota: a famous battle in which João I of Portugal defeated Juan of Castile on 14 August 1385.*

Following Page - Rua Dir

PILLORY

This is an ancient monument of great interest. It was used to punish delinquents and criminals in bygone days.

1 *Chafariz de Dona Catarina (Infanta Catherine's Fountain), Pillory and Porch*
2 *Chafariz de Dom João V ("João V's Fountain")*
3 *Chafariz do Arrabalde ou da D. Maria ("Infanta Maria's Fountain")*

AQUEDUCT AND FOUNTAINS

Catherine of Austria, spouse of João III, financed the construction of the aqueduct to supply the local fountains. The aqueduct is an imposingly high structure with a length of three kilometres and a large number of solid arches.

She ordered the *Chafariz de Dona Catarina* ("Queen Catherine's Fountain") to be built opposite the *Igreja de Santa Maria* (Saint Mary's Church).

The aqueduct also supplied water to the *Chafariz do Arrabalde* or "Fountain of Dona Maria".

The construction of another fountain, next to the *Santuário do Senhor da Pedra,* was commissioned in the reign of João V.

IGREJA MATRIZ DE SANTA MARIA (SAINT MARY'S PARISH CHURCH)

The *Igreja Matriz de Santa Maria* (Saint Mary's Parish Church) combines beauty and majesty and is Óbidos's most important edifice.

The church stands in the square opposite the fountain and pillory.

This Visigothic construction was built in the 8th century. It was converted into a mosque at the time of the Moors and returned to the Christians after the reconquest.

The church's inner walls are lined with blue and white tiles from the end of the 17th century. They are thought to be the work of Gabriel del Barco, who several authors consider to have been an Italian artist while others, Spanish.

The walls are adorned with large, beautiful paintings, depicting scenes from the gospels produced by Óbidos painter Baltazar Gomes Figueira.

The church has three naves. The ceiling is made from wood and is adorned with paintings from the late Renaissance period at the end of the 17th century.

The high altar has eight paintings on wood from the 17th century. They are thought to be the work of Óbidos painter João da Costa. The Annunciation, The Worship of the Shepherds, the Worship of the Three Wise Men, the Circumcision of the Infant Jesus, the Apostles next to the Virgin's Tomb pointing out to Saint Thomas, the place they had laid the body of Our Lady who had risen to heaven in body and soul, with the Assumption of the Virgin placed higher up.

Saint Catherine's Altar, to the right of the high altar displays five canvasses related with Saint Catherine by Josefa d'Óbidos, signed and dated 1661.

The upper canvasses depict Saint Teresa of Avila, Saint Francis of Assisi and the "Mystic Marriage of Saint Catherine". The central canvasses portray "Saint Catherine's Dispute with the Philosophers" and the "Destruction of the Catherine Wheel".

These are considered to be the painter's finest works, on the basis of their delicate brushwork, highly delicate details and polychromatic composition.

The inner walls separating the central nave are adorned with oil paintings on canvas, portraying scenes from the life of the Virgin Mary. They are thought to be the work of Josefa d'Óbidos or perhaps the "workshop" attributed to her, or even a negress who served her and who she taught to paint, owing to the fact that the canvasses are considered to be no more than passable.

The Tomb of João de Noronha the Younger, governor-general of Óbidos and his spouse Isabel de Sousa, lies on the northern side, to the left of the side altar of Our Lady of Sorrows.

This unusual and uniquely beautiful work of art, hewn from stone quarried in Ançã, is a

masterpiece of Coimbra's Renaissance period. The difficulty in attributing a construction date or identifying its artist derives from the fact that major refurbishment works were carried out on the church down the course of the centuries.

Several historians consider it to be the work of Jean de Rouen. Others consider it to be the work of Nicolau Chanterene.

In the centre of the tomb is a sculptural ensemble representing the Act of Laying the Body in the Tomb, whose most striking element is the Virgin Mother, holding the Dead Lord in her arms. The ensemble includes the figures of Saint John the Baptist and Saint Mary Magdalene.

JOSEFA D'ÓBIDOS

Josefa de Ayalla e Cabrera (1630-1684) was a famous painter. She usually went under the name of Josefa d'Óbidos and was an interesting figure in the Portuguese artistic scene of the 17th century.

She painted religious retables, panels for worship at home, was a portraitist, painter of coppers and miniatures, still-life scenes and, according to tradition, also modelled clay.

Several historians consider that she was born

in the Spanish city of Seville and that she moved to Portugal at the age of five. Others consider that she was actually born in Óbidos, lived in a provincial environment and spent her leisure time painting.

She passed away, in Óbidos, on 2 July 1684 and was buried in the *Igreja de S. Pedro* (Saint Peter's Church) according to the desires expressed in her last will and testament.

IGREJA
DA MISERICÓRDIA

The former *Capela do Espírito Santo* ("Chapel of the Holy Spirit"), currently known as the *Igreja da Misericórdia*, has a single nave, lined in tiles dating from the end of the 17th century.

The high and side altars depict the *Senhor dos Passos* ("Stages of the Cross") and our Lady of Sorrows with gilded carvings. The canvasses on the tribune, symbolise the "Visitation" and the "Advent of the Holy Spirit" by painter André Reinoso who is also considered to be the author of the canvasses "Christ Bearing the Cross" and "Christ on the Cross".

The tombstone which can be seen in the centre aisle is that of the 18th century Countess of Cavaleiros, Luísa Guerra.

IGREJA DE S. PEDRO
(SAINT PETER'S CHURCH)

This church, in times gone by, was classified as a basilica.

It was totally destroyed in the 1755 earthquake and rebuilt on top of a three nave gothic temple.

Its main chapel houses a highly ornate seventeenth century wood carved retable, depicting Saint Peter receiving the keys to Heaven from Christ.

The retable is thought to be the work of 17th century Óbidos painter, João da Costa.

The grave of the renowned painter Josefa d'Óbidos is thought to lie under the floorboards at the entrance to the sacristy, next to the side altar of Our Lady of the Rosary.

SANTUÁRIO DO SENHOR DA PEDRA

The church cannot be classified in architectural terms. It comprises several styles of which special reference should be made to its hexagonal shape.

The church has an image of the *Senhor da Pedra* (stone Christ), a rough hewn sculpture but none-the-less interesting for being so, on display in a glass cabinet on the high altar.

The church has "Twelve Apostles", comprising eight statues and four statuettes.

The canvasses adorning the church are thought to be the work of Vieira Portuense.

Reference should be made to the interesting tiled panels on the high altar's side walls.

PROCESSIONS

Óbidos is a medieval town with a highly religious ambience and particularly so during Holy Week.

Special reference should be made to the solemnity of the religious processions, in Óbidos, as they wind their way down its streets.

MUNICIPAL MUSEUM

This building used to be the premises of the town council. It was rebuilt at the behest of João IV and later converted to a prison. It now houses the municipal museum after the completion of major refurbishment works.

The museum has a collection of paintings, sculptures, sacred art and archaeological items in addition to weaponry dating back to the time of the Peninsular War.

ÓBIDOS BETWEEN WALLS.
A PEARL OF WESTERN PORTUGAL

A visitor who goes for a leisurely stroll through Óbidos is enveloped by the ambience of this pearl of western Portugal.

Sections of wall, narrow, winding medieval streets, *Manueline* style windows, picturesque recesses, rough-hewn steps, steep inclines, fascinating doors, austere façades, Moorish, medieval and hughly characteristic houses, arches, irregularly shaped roofs, all kinds of chimneys and an enormous diversity of flowers, carefully planted in flowerbeds bordered by stones, in red and lilac hue, in contrast with the whiteness of the blue or yellow striped houses which create a sensation that art and nature have united to enrich and embellish the town.

ÓBIDOS - A MEDIEVAL TOWN LOCATED IN A BEAUTIFUL SETTING

Óbidos is located in Estremadura, in a transition zone between north and south.

It occupies an arid, bare hill. Its inhabitants, in times gone by, reclaimed the land from the sea, creating agricultural and forest areas.

The region has a temperate, healthy climate with mild temperatures and moderate rainfall.

The value of the land between Óbidos and the Atlantic coast has naturally risen. Various crops were grown here, in abundance, such as cereals, vegetables, olive oil, wine and fruit. There was an abundant supply of fish and game owing to the various water courses meandering their way down through the forests into the lagoon. These are currently little more than rivulets which can hardly be made out among the vegetation but which, in more far off times, represented an important means of local travel for the inhabitants.

According to tradition, there was intense movement of vessels in the Middle Ages between the foot of the hill of Óbidos and the Atlantic, along the banks of the lagoon.

Sailors took their bearings from illumination provided by the *Torre do Facho* ("Torch-lit Watchtower").

The lagoon and rivers slowly silted up, putting an end to this commercial activity.

The geological features of the soil gave rise to other economic activities.

The region produces clay which naturally gave rise to clay modelling activities.

LAGOA DE ÓBIDOS (LAGOON)

Half a dozen kilometres to the west of Óbidos lies the lagoon (Lagoa d'Óbidos) comprising an expanse of water with an area of around 2,5 x 6 kilometres.

It flows into the Atlantic via a canal of varying breadth which is occasionally silted up in the summer months.

The River Arnóia and three other streams empty into the lagoon.

There used to be fish in abundance. Seaweed collecting, for use as a fertiliser was an activity of no less importance although people nowadays prefer to go fishing for clams and eels.

The lagoon is ideally suited to water sports.

It is enveloped by sparse clearings whose silence is only interrupted by the melodious chirping of birds which nest in the surrounding trees, with its reinvigorating atmosphere and still water, which elements help to create pleasant, restful settings and health-giving, enjoyable moments of rest.

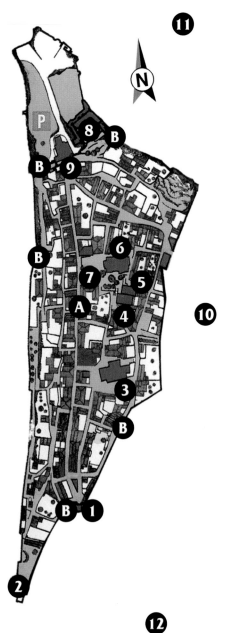

LEGENDS TO MAP

1 Entrance to Óbidos and Oratory Chapel (Our Lady of Piety)

2 Torre do Facho (Torchlit Tower)

3 Igreja de São Pedro (Saint Peter's Church)

4 Igreja da Misericórdia

5 Municipal Museum

6 Igreja Matriz de Santa Maria (Saint Mary's Parish Church)

7 Pelourinho, Chafariz de D. Catarina e Telheiro (Pillory, Queen Catherine's Fountain and poch)

8 Castelo, Pousada (Castle, Pousada)

9 Torre do Relógio ou Albarrã (Clock Tower or Barbican)

10 Chafariz do Arrabalde ou de D. Maria Chafariz do Arrabalde "Fountain of Dona Maria".

11 Chafariz de D. João V e Santuário do Senhor da Pedra "João V's Fountain" and Santuário do Senhor da Pedra (with a stone Christ)

12 Aqueduct

A Rua Direita

B Access to walls

ACKNOWLEDGMENTS

I wish to dedicate this simple publication to God, my parents, my wife and all those who have aided me in my development.

My sincere thanks also go to my good and dear friend Carlos Gomes Pereira.

A word of appreciation for "artists", for whom I nurture special affection. I have come to realise that it is only with a great deal of effort and commitment that they externalise and perpetuate their feelings, with demonstrations full of creativity … endearingly so … and so often unheeded.

The photographic compilation took much time and effort. A long, careful look and consequent wait. These were highly satisfying moments which gave me immense satisfaction, allowing me to achieve unprecedented personal fulfilment.

I apologise for any faults or if the overall result wasn't quite as good as I intended. It wasn't deliberate. I did my very best.

Óbidos is a very simple town. That's what makes it so beautiful.

I hope to have piqued your curiosity and that you'll want to come and visit.

Best regards.